D138663

Juggling for
a degree

Juggling for a degree

Mature Students' Experience of University Life

Edited by
Hilary Arksey
Ian Marchant *and*
Cheryl Simmill

Innovation in
Higher Education Series

Unit for Innovation
in Higher Education
School of Independent Studies
Lancaster University
Lancaster LAI 4YN

First published in 1994 by the Unit for Innovation in Higher Education, School of Independent Studies, Lancaster University, Lancaster LA1 4YN

ISBN 0 901800 49 X

PRINTED ON
RECYCLED PAPER

*Cover design by Rowland & Hird, Lancaster
Printed in Great Britain by Markprint,
Preston, Lancashire*

Contents

Preface by the Series Editor

B y the year 2000 Britain will have transformed its elite universities and colleges into a system of mass higher education. With expansion of student numbers and broadening of access it has become increasingly important to understand life at today's universities and colleges, too frequently presented in outdated stereotypes.

So, we are looking for first-hand accounts of experience at the modern university or college of traditional and modern teaching and assessment methods. We would be interested in accounts of all aspects of these institutions such as issues of race, class, age or gender; success and failure; finance; social life and the problems faced by those combining study with jobs and family responsibilities. Appreciation of these issues is crucial not only for students wishing to make the most of their higher education but also for the success of tutors and other staff in providing it.

If you are already – or about to be – involved in higher education in any way, as a student, professor, lecturer, research worker or other staff, we would like to invite you to consider describing and analysing your experience of today's higher education for publication in this series.

John Wakeford

Acknowledgements

We would like to thank the numerous people involved in the preparation of this book. Special thanks go to Janet Elleray, Liz Hampson, Kay Roscoe and Bron Szerszynski for taking time off from their studies to comment on an earlier draft of the text. We would also like to thank Linda Cook for the word processing of the manuscript. It has taken many months of hard work and rewriting to bring the book to a conclusion. We hope the end product gives you an insight into university life as experienced by a small number of mature students.

Hilary Arksey
Ian Marchant
Cheryl Simmill

Notes on Contributors: Why Are We Here? Does There Need to be a Reason?

The following short paragraphs give some indication about the different motivating forces which prompted the book's various authors to return to higher education.

Hilary Arksey:

Somehow, it just seemed a natural progression. Teaching in a college of further education got in the way of my Open University studies. When an opportunity arose to return to the other side of the desk as a full-time undergraduate student at Lancaster, I thought long and hard about exchanging what many people would consider to be a 'good career' for an unknown future; a future which at the time I saw as lying in the field of management in industry or commerce. A high risk strategy, a challenge, call it what you will, it was nevertheless a decision I haven't regretted.

Steve Barnes:

I'm at Lancaster as part of a calculated career move, I need to qualify in Social Work. There are many restrictions placed upon the unqualified Social Worker. You cannot practice Field Social Work nor can you become a Probation Officer. Also you cannot become legally involved with your clients.

Lynne Boundy:

Why **am** I here? It's a question I constantly ask myself as I slave over my word processor attempting to write essays on such esoteric subjects as ethnomethodology whilst everyone else is down at the pub. It isn't to open up new career opportunities, not with the short-sighted but prevailing view that anyone over 40 has a seizure when faced with a computer and can no longer count beyond 20. It isn't even the empty nest syndrome - I had a satisfying job and social life. I suppose the answer is that I'm here to prove to myself that I can do it.

John Clarkson:

As a pre-teenager, one of the questions you grow to hate is the one that well-meaning adults, uncles, aunts, and 'friends of the family' always throw at you when they run out of childish conversation: "What are you going to be when you grow up?" After the passage of many years, when you announce your intention of becoming a mature university student, your audience's reaction will instantly transport you back to that time.

"But what are you doing it for?" they will ask, looking at you the way your granny used to. Knowing that they would laugh if you were to say "Because I have a dream," you will mumble something vague and non-committal like, "I quite fancy teaching ...", and hope they'll go away. In truth, of course, hidden behind this new, polite, enquiry is still the same old question: "What are you going to be when you grow up?"

Even after graduation some of us are no nearer to finding an answer to that (but we have learned to stop worrying about it).

Ian Marchant:

After spending my 20s trying to become a pop star, I realised that I was too old, and spectacularly unsuccessful. Changed family circumstances dictated that I find a proper job, and I enrolled on a full-time engineering foundation course. I quickly realised that I stood as much chance of becoming an engineer as a pop star; I therefore applied to study the History of Science at University. Surely, I reasoned, there must be jobs for Historians of Science. Besides, I was bound to get a First.

Diane Nutt:

I used to work in a bookshop on a university campus. For seven years I watched hundreds, maybe thousands, of students, buy books and make the most (or worst) of their time at university, eventually coming out with degrees. I finally decided I'd had enough. I wanted to be on the other side of the counter. Well here I am and I love it. I would not go back behind that counter for anything. I love being a student.

Stuart Rose:

I came to University as a mature student not just for the enjoyment of my course - although it is very enjoyable - but to change my direction. Being an undergraduate is the first stage. Becoming a postgraduate research student is the planned second stage. My idea is to end up doing something a little more valuable than (in advertising) persuading housewives to buy one brand of detergent rather than another.

Cheryl Simmill:

Ever since I left school I have attended one kind of night class or another. Some of them were tedious, like shorthand and typing, whilst others were fun to do. O-level Archaeology for instance. However, I was quite surprised when an Open College tutor asked me why I was not applying for university. The thought hadn't crossed my mind. Surely university was for bright, young people, not people who had been in employment for twelve years? It was a difficult choice to give up a job I loved to turn a hobby into a lifestyle ... but I think it has been one of my better decisions.

Sara Winterbourne:

I can still clearly remember the moment I decided to go to university to get a degree. Sitting in a campaign meeting in a London advertising agency, discussing ideas for the launch of a new product. I kept counting up to twenty, trying to get up my confidence to break into the talk to voice my contribution. Looking round the room, it seemed to me that the others were all graduates, and so believed in themselves and their ideas. I decided that I would go to university, and prove to myself I was bright too!

Introduction

This book is a collection of personal narratives, each contributor presenting an account of one particular aspect of the mature student experience interspersed with practical managing techniques. The topic areas focused on are those which a straw poll, amongst the writers and other interested people, indicated were of primary concern. The idea originated out of a discussion about the highs and lows of academic life as experienced by your older-than-average student![1] It seemed to us that there was little, if any, information available describing what life in academia was *really* like: how it was perceived by mature students themselves, those brave (or foolhardy, depending on your viewpoint) creatures who had abandoned their past for new and unfamiliar pathways. *Juggling for a Degree* represents our attempts to fill this gap: testimonies written at the grass roots level by undergraduate and postgraduate students alike.

Perhaps the idea conveyed most strongly by the various contributions is that there is no common denominator in mature students' experiences. In this sense, it seems to us of little consequence that authors are concentrated on one campus; although specific to Lancaster University, we have no reason to believe our observations are not applicable to institutions in other parts of the UK. Indeed, it may well be that there is only one characteristic which applies to all mature students, and that

---

[1] In 1991 in the UK, 15.1 per cent of students successfully completing their studies were aged 25 or over. The percentage of mature students at universities was 12.4 compared with 19 per cent of graduates over 25 at the then polytechnics *(Older Graduates Statistics, 1991; Association of Graduate Careers Advisory Services: Sheffield Hallam University).*

is that they are those people who are over 21 years of age at the time of their entry to university. Diversity then is a key feature and we have attempted to illustrate this by including at the end of each piece comments from 'Other Voices', which put forward contrasting perspectives, viewpoints, suggestions and the like. This seemed to be the most effective way to get across a sense of (un)representativeness in the knowledge that the 'typical' mature student appears to exist only as a figment of the imagination. It's reassuring to know that difference is 'normal'.

Some overlaps, nevertheless, do emerge in the different contributors' writings. Mature students, it seems, tend to have their 'other lives' always present with them, more so than conventional-aged students. In this way, extra-curricular activities concerning children, partners, elderly relatives and pets (cats in particular) appear to be always in the back of the mind. Thus, the university experience develops the skills of juggling commitments and loyalties in order to balance the demands of academic work, family and friends (not to mention the bank manager). Another thread running through a number of pieces is that of building up informal network structures. These are valued as a means to explore new ideas and concepts in a friendly environment, and also act to counterbalance the stresses of the just mentioned 'other lives'.

In the organisation of the material we have included short paragraphs at the beginning and the end of the book to indicate contributors' initial reasons for taking a degree and their present intentions respectively. This comparison is intended to demonstrate how just being a student *changes* people. The first substantial piece outlines alternative routes for admission to university. This is followed by an account describing a day in the life of a mature student. The various issues alluded to here are then elaborated on individually in the narratives which follow. Subject areas include family and personal relationships; academic work requirements; social life; finance; health and ill health. The final piece looks at life after university and discusses possible options following graduation.[2] We conclude the book with lists of recommendations for firstly, mature students, secondly, teaching staff, and thirdly, academic institutions, based on our experience at University.

In sum, the book attempts to serve many purposes: to be entertaining; to be reassuring; to be informative; to be useful; to provide a balanced picture in terms of the fun side and the serious side of a student's life. We could go on. Perhaps we have been over-ambitious in this respect. If the message comes across, however, that despite everything the overall experience of being a mature student is both positive and rewarding, we will feel we have achieved a measure of success.

---

[2] In the UK, first destinations of 1991 over-25 university graduates were as follows: permanent UK employment 49.4 per cent; temporary UK employment 3.4 per cent; further academic study 14.4 per cent; teacher training 6.5 per cent; other study 8.0 per cent; overseas employment 2.2 per cent; unemployed 11.4 per cent; not available 4.8 per cent *(Older Graduates Statistics, 1991; Association of Graduate Careers Advisory Services: Sheffield Hallam University)*.

Access, Preparation and Admission

by

Stephen Barnes

I left education at 16 with no qualifications and joined the Police Cadets. At 19, I transferred to the Police Force, but, unable to settle, I left, and took a job as a drayman. After fourteen years earning "big money", (not to mention the freebies), just after Christmas 1987 I was given six weeks notice of redundancy. My wife and both my daughters cheered, but I was devastated. For a time I considered teaching music. Some years previously, I had taken up the trombone, and become reasonably competent to the extent that I passed several music exams. After enquiring at a local college, I discovered that in order to teach I needed Maths and English GCSE's as well as a couple of A-levels. My wife and I decided that it would all be worthwhile, if I could find some work while I studied. I started work as a stacker truck driver, and within hours I had been promoted to acting foreman, within weeks to foreman, and within months to supervisor. The idea of teaching music disappeared. I was sent on a management training course, and was subsequently advised to study for a degree in Management with the Open University (OU).

Learning with the OU is very different from being taught and learning in full-time education. With the OU, apart from a small number of group sessions a year, you are an independent learner. You correspond with an allocated tutor and have books to read, in addition to the well known radio and television broadcasts. There are regular written assignments, which are marked, and then, returned with feedback, which, if you can understand your tutor's handwriting, can be extremely helpful. You have to be highly motivated and very patient to succeed with the OU. You could slog away at courses and get a BA in maybe four years, but most students take between six and eight years. It can be expensive too, at around £300 per course.

The Open College of the North West is a different route into higher education. The Open College has been running for several years locally and has proved to be very successful at introducing mature students into institutions of higher education. Being at Open College gives you the chance to discuss the subject with your tutor and fellow students. For many people the College is about confidence building and making friends with others who may well go into higher education at the same time as yourself. Therefore, the College becomes not only a place to study, but also a centre for socialising and building up networks.

Usually two Open College 'B' units are required for entry into university. You do not have to launch straight into 'B' units. If you wish to 'try out' a subject you can go on a sixteen week 'A' unit (not to be confused with A-levels), which costs £33.12. The 'B' courses are thirty-two weeks long and cost £74.55 (prices in September 1993).

Across the country there are a number of different systems available to mature students who wish to enter higher education. It is well worth contacting your local education authority to find out what is available.

Back to my own story now. Through the OU, I completed two-and-a-half courses in two years. By this time, though, I had decided on a complete change of direction. The OU course was supposed to further my career, which it did, so much so that I was expected to travel the country setting up contracts. I was reluctant to take on this sort of work, as I had no wish to leave my wife and children at home. Fortunately, I was able to get a full-time job working for Salford Social Services at a secure unit, which would give me a wealth of experience in Social Work, probation and prison work. I intended to run my academic life parallel to my working life, hoping that Salford would second me to do my Certificate of Qualification in Social Work (CQSW), which I needed for field social work. They were unable to do this; but, having completed a foundation course with the OU, and with my work experience, I knew that I could transfer to full-time education, and hopefully manage financially on a Local Education Authority grant. Wishing to qualify in Social Work/Probation, I found a number of options open to me, from two to four years in length. Apart from a commitment to Social Work, I had to demonstrate my academic ability at an interview; this is the same for any degree course. In addition, some colleges may require essays, or even written tests before admission.

I was lucky enough to be given an unconditional offer by Lancaster University on the strength of my interview. In the summer before taking up my full-time place, my department sent me a reading list; all courses should do this as a matter of routine. If they don't, then ring your department and nag them for one. Having now completed my first year back in full-time education, I can honestly say that my time with the Open University provided me with a range of study skills which have proved invaluable. What it did not prepare me for was the freedom of a university education. Perhaps, for an ex-cop, this is the biggest shock of all.

Other Voices say:

"I got here through the Open College. ... the whole exercise seems to be a confidence builder ... out of real life into adult education ..."

"I went to a job centre. I found a prospectus for Lancashire Polytechnic. ... I took a woman's course ... I needed to get my confidence back ... From this I needed something more stimulating ... I came to Lancaster ..."

"Nothing is written in tablets of stone; there are as many routes in as there are students. Two favourite examples are that of a friend who was accepted on the strength of her interview alone, without having studied anything at all for fifteen years; and that of another friend who was accepted onto a postgraduate MA course without being a graduate, or having undergone any kind of further education. In both cases, work experience was the deciding factor which gained them admittance to university."

"I did a Geography A-level at night class, really to see if I could enjoy studying again. I enjoyed it, but it was not until I visited the University to see someone in the Adult Education Office that I really decided to go for it. I was told that I'd need two courses, so in addition I took computing through the Open College, and I'm glad I did, because I felt it was very good preparation for what we're doing here."

"Academic work - I find it difficult. Open College was an exercise in giving you confidence. When I came up here I just wasn't prepared for the shock. I realised that there were certain academic standards I was going to find difficult to achieve. I haven't learned many lessons. I've just tried harder and harder."

A Life in the Day of a Mature Student

by

Lynne Boundy

I may not come out at the end of my three years at Lancaster University with a First Class Honours degree but I shall certainly be a skilful master in the art of spinning plates. Like all mature students who have a home and family, I spend my time in a vain attempt to resolve the conflict between the domestic and the academic. The time management books' are fine in theory but what they don't tell you is what to do when the word processor decides it's not going to print the last three pages of the essay that's due in tomorrow, the cat's just been sick and friends have 'phoned to say they're in the area, can they stay a couple of nights. I know the theory; this is the reality.

My radio alarm wakes me at seven o'clock - an ungodly hour, but I like to allow myself the luxury of half an hour in bed with the TODAY team to keep up with what's going on in the real world. However, this morning I have a lecture at nine o'clock which means leaving the house before eight to drive the forty-five miles to Lancaster - so TODAY will just have to do without me. (How I resent arriving on campus and seeing all those drawn curtains in the rooms of students who obviously drag themselves out of bed ten minutes before their first lecture!) Fortunately I no longer have to organise lunch boxes, PE kits, childminders and all those myriad things that mature students with young children have to contend with. I admire their fortitude. A quick shower, a dash round the kitchen with a slice of toast, take a cup of tea up to my teenage son (his turn tomorrow), glance at the headlines in the paper and grab my bag. I've learned to prepare myself the night before and make sure I have everything I need for the following day. There's nothing worse than arriving at a seminar without the notes you've so assiduously prepared, or going to the library and finding the definitive book to finish that essay you've been agonising over for so long, only to discover you've left your library card (and possibly your wallet) lying at home on the kitchen table. I make a mental note to buy catfood on the way home - have I enough money in my purse? I can make do with a coffee and a cigarette for my lunch, but the cat's somewhat fussier!

Into the car, put on a tape, switch on to automatic pilot, and then spend the next three quarters of an hour mentally organising my day. Whether that coincides with what really happens is another thing. After my first lecture I have a spare hour, then a seminar, another lecture and finally a seminar at three. I've given up trying to work on campus. The odd free hours between lectures are never long enough to achieve anything constructive, except to take advantage of the library resources, see tutors or just talk to people - though, as Diane later points out, talking can be as profitable as anything else. After all, isn't university life about exposing oneself to new ideas, challenging received wisdom and becoming involved in debate and discussion? Sometimes it's easy to think that it's just about getting good marks in assignments and passing exams. Today I must use my free time to look for a book I need for an essay. It's the perennial problem of too many students chasing too few books. Ideally I shall be able to get it from Short Loan but that entails being back on campus for ten o'clock next morning when my first lecture isn't until twelve. I wonder how part-time students manage? Maybe I can photocopy what I want, if it doesn't involve waiting in a queue while half a dozen other people copy what looks like the entire Encyclopaedia Britannica?

One o'clock - two lectures and a seminar later - I have the choice of spending an hour in thought-provoking conversation over a coffee or attending an academic skills session on *How to Improve Your Essay Writing*. On balance the essay writing wins. It's also an opportunity to share your concerns and realise that you're not the only one who panics when faced with a blank sheet of paper. What happened to all that confidence I had at 18? Have those years of nappy changing and attending the needs of others atrophied my brain? I sometimes envy 18 year-olds for whom essay writing is a way of life.

Finally at four o'clock I decide I've had enough so back on to automatic pilot and the journey home. At first the idea of spending two unproductive hours a day driving affronted my protestant work ethic so I had visions of taping my lectures and playing them back in the car. Alas, all I got was a recording of twenty students coughing. Now I regard that time as my own personal space when I can reflect on my day, mull ideas over in my mind about a forthcoming project or just indulge in some fantasy about where I'm going at the end of all this - given the economic situation, probably where I was before I started! I did use the time to advantage at the end of my first year when I put my revision notes on to tape and listened to them in the car before my exams.

Five o'clock and I'm home again - just like anyone else's working day really, except I know I ought to spend another three hours reading and making notes. My son, who's taking his A-levels, is already in his room doing his homework. After three previous attempts and years of nagging my older offspring to work harder, I finally got one who's conscientious. There's now a role reversal and he nags me when my latent hedonism takes over and I'm tempted to spend the evening watching television. We exchange notes about our day while I produce something for supper based on a thousand and one ways with mince or "What shape pasta shall we have tonight?" Having done the Earth Mother bit in a previous existence, I now realise that bought cakes and the odd frozen pizza don't actually produce juvenile delinquents, and that with a monthly supermarket shop and plentiful supplies of fresh fruit and vegetables we can have a healthy diet without my spending hours in the kitchen.

A couple of 'phone calls to the aforementioned offspring to assure them that they're not forgotten and, of course, I'd love to see them (and their washing) and two of their flatmates for the weekend, but I really need to get my head round post-structuralism so they'll have to fend for themselves. I don't tend to work on Saturdays. That's generally written off to domestic pursuits, the shopping and the laundry and the little bit of housework I do to salve my conscience, though the notice I have in the kitchen saying A TIDY HOUSE IS A SIGN OF A WASTED LIFE serves to assuage the guilt! I also try to keep up with friends I had in my previous life so perhaps we'll go to the cinema or share a bottle of wine on Saturday evening. Sundays are usually assigned to work, unless the weather's particularly good when I might attack the garden with a machete.

My stroke of genius has been to organise my timetable so that I have one day a week when I don't have to go to Lancaster. That is invaluable as it allows me a whole day without interruptions to catch up on essay writing, allowing, of course, for all the delaying tactics like reading the newspaper from cover to cover, doing the crossword, 'phoning all my friends, cleaning the oven, and all the really pressing things which need to be done before I can start.

Finally I retire to bed about half-past eleven with the thoughts of Noam Chomsky - guaranteed to send anyone to sleep. (I'll catch up with all those novels in the summer vacation.) I drift off to sleep reflecting on the holiday I'm going to have - if I manage to pay all those bills and get a job to support me in the summer. And if I don't, I'll just have to go and stay with my various offspring and treat them like a hotel. It's my turn now.

Other Voices say:

"If you have a family, you may not be able to work at any time, but it is best to decide early on how to find time to work and where. A friend who has children spends two days on campus at seminars and working in the library while her children are in the creche, and three evenings a week her husband looks after them while she works at home. Any other time she needs she negotiates shared child care with a friend, so they each have free afternoons or mornings to work. It sounds complicated, but it makes life so much easier if you can sort out some sort of pattern early on. Having said all that, life is never neat and you have to remain flexible, but having a system organised in the first place makes any changes much more manageable."

"There are ways and means of completing work during vacation periods, (dissertations are just one example) instead of being limited to the official (ten week) terms, which can end up extremely intense and concentrated."

"In our house the microwave has become a firm family friend and our use of tinned foods produces almost enough metallic waste to support the entire recycling industry."

"Delaying tactics! From desperately needing to go to the loo (pausing only to select some suitable - non-academic - reading material) all the way to examining the dog's teeth (honestly!). I reckon this topic alone would fill several volumes."

"My biggest problem is that I've got to work whenever I'm free. I can't choose; I can't say "Oh, I'll do it next week" because I don't know what's going to happen. I've just got to work whenever I can. And so I do."

"At one stage I would feel there was something amiss if I didn't wake up in the morning and feel the weight of a book on my chest."

"... many mature students describe the experience as 'plate spinning' and if one plate comes tumbling down then it threatens all the others. It is often at these times that you look for the support of your partner. However one cannot always rely on their immediate help. It may well be that they too are under some kind of extra stress and feel unable to bail you out."

"Personally I have tried to structure my work around an 'average week'. However when something happens, for example if someone is ill, then academic work has to be put on hold. In the past I have felt frustrated and guilty because I have not done the work allotted to that time. Time management courses only compounded the problem. These days I acknowledge that it is not easy and that at the end of the day you can only do your best, which to be honest, is often enough!"

Teamwork

by

John Clarkson

It is difficult to explain the impact that cinema had on children of my generation, except to say that, in the 1950s, to walk like Robert Mitchum, sneer like Humphrey Bogart, do one's hair like Tony Curtis and to kiss girls in the same way that Errol Flynn did, was part of normal behaviour. Although we knew that the movies were only fantasy, the images they presented were so powerful, so persuasive and, above all, so different from our everyday lives, that much of our pubescent life seemed to be spent in a constant struggle to make unruly hormones conform to the tenets of the unwritten moral code which ruled on-screen relationships.

In cinematic convention, English universities were sunny, ivy-clad utopias, where relaxed students drove vintage Bentleys, wore long scarves, drank endlessly without getting drunk, and had sexless liaisons with Muriel Pavlow. Study, if mentioned at all, was a minor, but painless irritant. For me, it was love at first sight. Me and university were made for each other. To hell with the Americanised drawl and leer; the urbanity, savoir-faire and devil-may-care-ness that came from a university education were what really counted in life. But the course of love, just like in the movies, never did run smooth. I had a living to earn. Consummation would have to wait a while.

I did all the right (conventional) things, worked hard, reached the top, got used to the flash company car and expense account lunches: I was a success. The idea of university still surfaced occasionally, but as a nostalgic memory rather than a realistic possibility. As the dream receded, so I felt more and more trapped, as though all my options in life had been removed. Business life was providing all the material trappings but no real satisfaction. Home was the place where I slept; my family a group of people my wife would tell me about. Our ignorance of each other's lives was mutual. While I bitterly resented our separation, the only compensation I could offer was more money, earned by working longer hours.

The decision to start my own business was, I think, tied in with the idea that, as my own boss, I might get more free time (as well as earning more money). Predictably, I spent even more time nurturing my business, but my income grew, and as it did, so did the awareness that neither I, my wife nor my children were really happy. Now my dream about university recurred more often, but always with regret, as something I had missed and now would never get the chance to try. My business lasted for six years, the last two of which were a desperate struggle to keep my drowning venture afloat. Finally, when I felt that I could go on no longer, I realised that there was the possibility of life after failure, and that all I needed was the courage to wind up the business and admit defeat. Within days I had done just that. The relief was unbelievable. My family were delighted. For the first time in years I felt relaxed.

After a few weeks at home, the question 'what now?' started to become more pressing. My wife brought things to a head one morning while we were having breakfast: "You've been going on about university for years; now's your chance. You know you can do it and so do we, so stop feeling sorry for yourself, get off your backside and do something about it." Stung, I picked up the 'phone and rang the local Adult College to ask their advice, and was amazed to find just how easily they accepted the idea that someone like me should want to go to university. The euphoria soon wore off. Having been presented with a plan of action by the College, all sorts of misgivings began to surface. In the family discussions which took place, I raised every objection I could find, pointing out the likely cost to them of my actions. They were firm. This would be my only chance. They didn't want me to go back to being the money-obsessed workaholic stranger I had been, they wanted back the father they had had before 'business' had taken over my life. In the face of my objections, they dredged up every bit of support they could find for their *'Get Father to University'* campaign. Overwhelmed, I gave in and took the College course that Lancaster University required.

By the time I actually entered Lancaster, our meagre savings had run out and it seemed we would have to rely almost totally on the Local Education Authority grant. As we were soon to find out, what it didn't allow for was the 'unconsidered trifles': all those silly little things which help relieve the occasional monotony of life and which, like everyone else, we had taken for granted. My daughters took part-time jobs, my wife - herself studying for a History Diploma - earned extra money by sewing. I, driven by my guilt, found a casual, part-time job in my old sphere, even though I felt that I had no time to spare. Each day the tension in the house grew, there were days when no-one spoke to anyone else except in curt monosyllables. The dogs cowered perpetually. The cats appeared only at their meal-times.

The day when everything exploded was a memorable one, with everyone shouting at everyone else, and each complaining of the others' insensitivity, laziness, selfishness and a long list of other, more or less heinous, character defects. Only when things had calmed down and tears been dried were we able to discuss, relatively calmly, what had happened. The root cause of our problem had, it seemed, been a growing resentment by each of us about everyone else's meagre input into the running of the house in comparison with our own. I was resented for being home most of the time, and yet failing to keep the house tidy. Spending my time reading was not perceived as 'working'. My wife was resented for the way she tried to organise everyone else into housework without, it was felt, including sufficient duties for either me or herself. I resented the children for their reluctance to do any work in the house without hassle, and my wife for not understanding the pressures I was under; she resented me for the way I misunderstood both her and the children. Each of us resented the unappreciated sacrifice of study time which our paid job represented. By a process which was a blend of negotiation and public confession, we managed nervously to hammer out a sort of treaty, in which we all vowed to voice our irritations in future before they got out of hand. Along with this went an agreement that we would each try to show more consideration to everyone else and, in particular, not expect from anyone a more zealous attitude toward housework than one was prepared to show oneself.

There have been arguments since that time, of course, often bitterly emotional ones too, but they have all (so far) proved capable of resolution. The idea of living in a 'democratic family' was difficult at first for me, since my idea of family life had always been more than a little Victorian. However, our commitment to freedom of speech (with only a few limitations) has given all of us a much more relaxed attitude towards old conventions. The house is rather dusty and universally untidy, but nobody gets uptight about it any more. My wife and I are certainly more unkempt than formerly. As for the kids, well the two girls are both away at university, so coming home is just like an extension of their daily life. Our 14 year-old son always did think that we were slightly unhinged so what he sees every day simply confirms that view. What is important, is that we are happy. I got my degree, and was so enthusiastic (or lazy) that I came back to do postgraduate work. My wife is currently studying for her first degree. There are still problems, both emotional and financial, but we're all better able to cope than we used to be. As a family, our earlier traumas have taught us a lot about how to survive, how to talk to each other, how to show support - and love.

It hasn't been easy, but it's been worthwhile. My only regret is that I didn't do it sooner; while I was still young enough to wear the long scarf, drive the Bentley, and buy Muriel Pavlow a drink or two.

Other Voices say:

"When I was in full-time employment my partner used to ask me about my work: "How was it going?", "What was I doing?" Since I have been at University he has not asked. He has stated that he is not interested in academic arguments as he lives in 'The Real World' and I do not."

"I feel our relationship would not have been so interesting if I had not attended University."

"An apocryphal tale from my first year concerns the English tutor, who, in his first lecture, said that anyone who was married would be divorced by the end of their course. I laughed when I heard this story; except that, by the end of my course, I was, if not divorced, then separated from my wife, who had worked throughout the whole of my three years. The demands we made on one another were unsustainable. My wife, looking for a new start, decided to go to university; as a graduate, I started looking for a job. By the end of her first year, we understood one another much better. And now we're house-hunting together."

"My partner is not an academic so there were lots of times when he did not know what I was talking about. It was difficult ... it was not that he was not interested ... In the end I decided to keep things separate: my family on one side and my academic work on the other."

"My postgraduate studies have drawn me closer to my parents. In their eighties, they are rapidly becoming experts in Repetitive Strain Injury (RSI), my thesis topic, and are the ones telling me about new developments in the medical controversy, sending me newspaper cuttings, magazine articles and the like. It's the same with my children, but in their case it tends to be in terms of television programmes. My PhD is developing into a collaborative family project."

On Being a Mature Student with Children

by

Cheryl Simmill

A friend once said that major life changes come about every seven years ... it's something to do with the return of Saturn. Personally I was rather sceptical about this concept until I hit my twenty-eighth birthday. At this point Saturn returned with a vengeance. Within a year I changed from being a single, career woman into a Mum and a student ... a change, which up to now, I have not regretted ... although it has had its difficult patches!

After only a couple of days on the campus, it dawned on me that there were quite a number of older people around - and they were not all teaching staff. Quite a high percentage of the mature students seemed to have children of one age or another, including one 'fresher' who was a great-grandmother! There are many ways of getting to know people when you first arrive on campus and in my case carrying Becky around, my four month-old daughter, did the trick.

It soon became clear that I was not the only one with a young baby, as several parents of very young children gathered at the Pre-School Centre. The intake at the Centre was very carefully managed by the staff, although pressures on places did not make the situation ideal at times. Meanwhile the babies were totally oblivious to the comings and goings of their parents, as they built up a strong bond with the nursery nurses and each other. It was a great relief to know that your child was totally content whilst you were doing battle with the books!

However, for those students with children of pre-school and school age, the effects of any problem can be immediate and, at times, dramatic. Illness in the family causes panic bells to ring when you are trying to complete course work. A friend recently commented that she would do almost anything to get to her lectures and felt guilty at having to lean on friends and relatives for child care in order to do so. I think the majority of student-parents feel like this at some time or other.

There are times when the whole experience is a bit of a juggling act, or like the line of dominoes: once one falls, down they all go. On the whole the student-parents I have met have been dedicated to all the activities in their lives: to family, friends, external commitments and concerns. This can result in either a series of variously weighted 'boxes' of activities, or, as in my case, the whole thing blurring into one experience.

Much of my degree scheme took the experience of being a parent into account. I could spend days reading up on the theoretical interactions between child care policy and paid employment, just to have the whole thing blown apart during a five minute practical lesson! Becky, at under three and still very dependent on me, was a constant reminder of the everyday practicalities of life. She frequently brought me down to earth with a bump from the dizzy heights of academic theory ... an experience every academic should, and probably does, go through.

Being a student-parent certainly keeps you on the move as there is no getting away from your responsibilities. An 'average day' can start to look like a series of 'track events'. The early morning jog to drop the children off at school or the child minder's; the sprint for the bus or through the traffic to get on campus; a relay of lectures, library, seminar, library, with a final hurdle back to collect the children. Personally the half-a-mile run down from the main campus and back up to lectures, four times a day, certainly kept me going. However, what was gained in exercise was lost in stress!

In spite of the 'parent olympics' some parents do get involved in 'off-track' events. Several parents at Lancaster University got together to form a Student-Parent Group called SProG. It was our aim to make the University aware of the practical problems facing · students who had the added responsibility of being parents, especially of young children. One major problem for mature students with children is that of finding a home. Unfortunately the Accommodation Office is not geared up to helping mature students with families find a house. It would seem that children are equated with pets when it comes to rented accommodation - 'No children, no pets.' Our campaigns were for simple, practical solutions to everyday problems. We did not want to be seen as calling for preferential treatment, just asking for a few measures to put us on a more equal footing with the other students. For example one of the campaigns was for a bus stop near the Pre-School Centre; another was for a nappy changing facility on campus. It took some time, but through a little pressure and lobbying on committees we achieved the nappy changing room and the new Pre-School Centre will be very near to the main campus bus stop.

It is often said that when you have children the problems don't go away, they just change. This is certainly the case as the children leave Pre-School facilities and go on to local schools. At the very least the Pre-School facilities covered the hours and terms of the University, unlike the usual school hours. As more and more lectures are scheduled later into the day, to accommodate the growing numbers of students, things are going to become more difficult for the student with school-aged children. Limited school hours, the general lack of holiday and after-school care nationally is only compounded by the presence of the occasional 'Baker Day' which always seems to appear just when you least need it. Obviously these problems are not specific to student-parents but to all parents in Britain today. We are fortunate at Lancaster in having a Students' Union which is aware of the student-parent dilemma and has organised a half-term play scheme for Primary and Junior school-aged children. However, this still leaves the question of what is best for older children.

On reflection there would appear to be little difference between being a parent, working either at home or in paid employment, and being a student-parent. There are all the familiar problems of finding good quality and consistent child care facilities, for both pre-school and school-aged children, as well as trying to complete the tasks you have to do. There have been times when I have thought that it would be easier to stay at home with Becky, than to have all the hassle of doing a degree. However, the long summer vacation always reminds me about the reality of being a full-time mum, at home, alone, with a young child. This is not a one-way process. In the past Becky has left me in no doubt about where she would rather be!

On Graduation Day I received a certificate telling me that I had got a degree: that I had done well. It felt worth the effort; I was floating on air. Then Becky asked me why I was wearing a Batman cape and a silly hat. People congratulated me and shook my hand, saying that it must have been difficult with a young child around. Yes it was ... but not half as difficult as being a Mum, and you don't get a certificate saying 'Successful Parent' do you?

Becky is now four and has just started school. One of her Pre-School friends has gone with her. Her life is changing at a steady pace as she moves from being a toddler to a very

.independent young person. As for me ... well I'm still enjoying my Saturn return doing postgraduate research and wondering what the next seven years may hold for me.

> **Other Voices say:**

"When I started to do my degree my two boys were 8 and 11 years-old. They were at the age when children start to think that their parents know nothing, so I was glad to be able to point out that I too was involved in the learning process. I also felt that being at the University kept me in touch with young people: their music, fashion, what they thought.

However, the situation also had its drawbacks. My sons were too old for child minders and too young to be left alone. I always had to leave University at 3.00 pm to make sure that I was back in time to meet them from school. This often meant that I missed lectures and other events, like Students' Union meetings that were held later in the day. I also found that it was often 9.30 pm before I could get down to doing my 'homework' after helping my sons with theirs! 'Baker Days' and half-term holidays were also difficult to manage, as my sons were too old for the play scheme run by the Students' Union. This meant that I had to resort to taking a week off (ie away from the university) to cover for these 'holidays'."

"My son was introduced to 'university' when he was about 13 or 14. Until that point, he had no idea what the word meant. By occasionally coming to campus with me he discovered that, as well as books and teachers and studying, university also encompassed pool tables and video game machines and bars and the sports centre and shops: a whole way of life. He is now much better informed as to whether or not he wants to follow in my footsteps."

"I feel that by being a parent I missed out on the social life ... that's all really. Looking back, I do wonder if I neglected my children to some extent, especially with having to do placements over the holiday periods."

"Both of my sons had a role model, someone working, studying, doing it for their own reasons which may have set a standard for them ... to help them decide what they want."

"One of my sons went on to university, whilst I was completing my degree, and the other decided to take A-levels. However, I sometimes wonder if I have given them unrealistic expectations."

Surviving Academic Work

by

Diane Nutt

Why should I have anything significant to say about academic work? Well, I'm not sure anything I have to say is necessarily significant, but I could certainly talk about it forever! I am totally obsessed by work. Now don't get me wrong, I am not a swot (whatever that might be), I'm just a third year! It isn't that finals are on the horizon, rather I am actually tripping over them.

The first thing I'd like to say about working, is how much more appealing writing this is than getting on with the essay I'm supposed to be doing. In fact how much more appealing anything is than writing essays, even the washing up! Having said that, whatever else you are doing, you spend 99 per cent of the time thinking about the academic work you have not done! Now, I might be wrong but this does seem to be more of a problem for mature students. Not because we do less work, but because most mature students have invested so much in being here. Also mature students can come up with infinitely more distractions.

I came to University with mixed feelings, the most dominant being excitement and fear. Excitement because I wanted to do everything as the Access course I had done to enable me to get here had only whetted my appetite; the fear, on the other hand, tended to overcome the excitement. I was afraid I would not be able to reach the standard of work expected; I was afraid I would not be able to contribute anything in seminars; I was afraid I would not understand the lectures. The bad days are when you get a low mark for an essay, or when an idea completely escapes you, or when everything and anything gets in the way of your work (your washing machine decides to spill gallons of water all over your kitchen; the cat is sick on your essay; your computer crashes; you've had a row with your partner). Fortunately, the bad days are outnumbered by the good: when you get a high mark for an essay; an encouraging comment from your tutor; a thank-you from a fellow student you have actually been able to help; when you suddenly understand something that has been eluding you forever; when you finish a piece of work; when you find the perfect quote for your next essay. Here are a few techniques which helped me to increase the good days.

First of all I have discovered that mature students have a lot to offer. If, like me, you have been in paid work before coming to university, you will have learned how to structure your life and your work, a valuable lesson when it comes to managing your academic life. Furthermore, mature students tend to bring a greater commitment to their work because we really want to be here, and we have often made sacrifices to do it. So value what you are and what you can give; have confidence in your own experiences.

Secondly, make contacts with others. Discussing your work with others is a good way to improve it. I also discovered reading each other's work, though initially nerve racking, is a great way to discover what is good about it as well as what isn't. Paying attention to tutors' comments on your work and trying to put their words into practice, talking to them about your work and taking their advice can only improve your work. Talking to others helps you realise you are not alone in your worries, almost everyone suffers the same (or similar) difficulties. Moreover, they may have discovered a solution you haven't thought of. If you are having problems, talk to someone, regardless of whether or not they are academically related. For many mature students it is everything else that proves a problem, which then goes on to affect your ability to work. When my life was getting in the way of my work, I found talking to my tutor was very helpful; we managed to rearrange my work around the crises. Likewise, friends have been very helpful by taking on some of my non-academic responsibilities when I have come up against inflexible deadlines. In sum, my second technique for survival is communication.

Thirdly, it helps to discover how you work best. Personally, I work best in the middle of the night, in my room, with the door shut so the cats cannot get in and I do not disturb anyone else in the house. I don't have a word-processor of my own, and so use the University facilities, and I do all my non word-processing work during my most productive working times and then spend a series of days every few weeks at a computer terminal at the University.

It is also worthwhile doing some work in any 'spare' time you might have, then, if and when the crisis occurs, you've something in hand. Most 18 year-olds seem to do their work at the very last minute under pressure; however appealing, it's much harder to do that if you have a lot of outside commitments. Personally, I have to admit I need to be under pressure to work effectively, so I either create my own deadlines or get my tutor or a friend to set them for me, often before the actual departmental deadline.

About exams - everyone worries about exams, EVERYONE. People might tell you they don't worry. Well, don't believe them. If they don't worry, they don't work and if they don't work, they worry. Worry is nature's way of psyching you up to work, or so I tell myself! I have found the best way to cope with exams is to get yourself organised well in advance, take advice on what you need to do, get on with it and when it comes to the day: you are going in with the information, plus a little bit of worry to get the adrenaline going, and you will be fine, honestly.

Finally, don't give up. There will undoubtedly be times for us all when everything appears so awful that it doesn't seem worth going on. Just keep going, tomorrow will not be as bad, and the day after will probably be wonderful, and you will want to be a student forever, I should know, I am seriously contemplating the prospect of postgraduate studies!

Other Voices say:

"I've really tried to be disciplined, looking at my studies in the terms of a job/career. I get on to campus as soon as possible after nine and stay until five o'clock. I've learned that lesson; you have to really apply yourself and set yourself targets. If you do that and treat it like a job, putting in a full day for five days of the week, then when you don't read in the evenings, or don't do any work at the weekends, you don't feel guilty about it because you've given it a fair crack during the week."

"My experience is that, for all sorts of reasons, I have not been able to communicate with other students to any great extent during the previous three years. This is partly because there are very few students following similar ideas to myself, and partly because of my inward-looking nature. The point I want to make is that being solitary is also OK - you can still have a very rewarding and enjoyable academic life."

"I find a change of scene helps me work in an indirect, intangible way. For instance, reading an article and then going out for a walk where I can mull all the ideas around in my head whilst out in the fresh air, sunshine and the like. This technique was especially useful when I was revising and preparing for exams. All-in-all, a good way of turning exercise into prime working time."

"It's the initial 'pen-to-paper'/'finger-to-keyboard' that is the most difficult step. There's a great tendency to carry on reading in order to put off the writing. It's important to know when to stop reading and when to start writing. Getting the introductory paragraph done is a great psychological step, the rest is far easier once that leap has been made."

Having Fun

by

Ian Marchant

By the time I decided to go to university, just before my thirtieth birthday, I had changed to such an extent that I really thought that I had lost my interest in sex 'n' drugs and rock 'n' roll. The old me was dead and buried. Probably, I thought, when I get to university, I'll be such an old sober sides, that the only people I'll be mates with will be sartorially challenged lecturers, and we'll sip dry white wine, and listen to Schoenburg, and rap about post-modernism. Or something.

So why, I asked myself on my first night at University, am I in the kitchen of a Hall of Residence with sixty 18 year-olds, who showed little or no interest in post-modernism, and a great deal of interest in getting very pissed and vomiting over people they had only just swapped A-level results with? More worrying still, I found myself approaching an 18 year-old hippy, and asking the perennial question of university first nights, namely, "Have you got any drugs?" "No," he said. (I later found out he was lying.) "Do you fancy trying to score?" I said. "Yes," he replied. This was the beginning of a beautiful relationship, one which has continued to this day. Over our first few weeks he introduced me to all his terrible 18 year-old friends, and everything seemed to be going swimmingly, until I remembered that I had just turned 30 and was a serious person, and that it was neither appropriate nor physically possible for me to drop Es and dance all night. I sought for more mature chums, and kept my contact with K and his mates to no more than two or three times a week.

One of the problems of meeting mature students is that it is not impossible to come across the odd soul mate, a slacker at heart, a person who always has less important things to do. A few mature students are retired party-goers for whom the grant, far from being a pittance on which they can hardly survive, represents a huge wad of free money. It can be difficult, therefore, when making mature student friends, to meet people who genuinely wish to be as sober as you do. It all starts to go horribly wrong in the coffee bar, after your seminar. Oh sure, you start with good intentions, rapping about post-modernism, and so on, but that leads on to stronger stuff, and within minutes you find yourself laughing at people's stories, and trying to top them with your own. Soon, somebody will complain about how crap their relationship is, and how their children don't understand them, and you are flooded with fellow feeling, and suddenly you are missing your lecture. Never mind that the 18 year-olds have missed them all, for you it seems like a big deal. Don't worry, the feelings of guilt will go. In no time at all, you find yourself arriving on campus at nine o'clock and sitting in your favourite coffee bar with your wrinkly pals all day, only moving for lunch and increasingly frequent trips to the lavatory. Beware of these people.

A great deal of mature student social life tends to be focused in college or on campus, and happens during the day, when one really should be in the library working. But the kids are in school or nursery, and one's partner is safely out of the way, and coffee, though its diuretic properties may cause problems this late in life, at least enables you to stay awake during those tricky post-lunch lectures. At night, mature students, who may live some way from the college, who may have child care problems, or partners who wish to continue their old, well established patterns of socialising, do not have the chance to be hectic on a major scale. Still, opportunities for fun do exist, and it is important that mature students try to grab them, whether it be a Mature Students Society disco or barbecue, or one night a week on the beer with your chums. Fun is central to the university experience.

One day, I was sitting harmlessly in the coffee bar when it occurred to me that some of the guys were old rockers, just like me: what is more, we practically had a viable line up just around our table! How we laughed! A week later, there we were, drums, bass guitar, sax, trumpet, vocals, rehearsing, and I was, at age 31, a member of a student rock band. A month later we were doing a gig. Last year, we supported The Bay City Rollers who were, if nothing else, at least older than us, and I thanked God for small mercies. No one much cares that we're not very good: it gets us out of the house, and into trouble. Through my return to the boards I ended up meeting lots of people: artists, who, having suffered our music, insisted that I suffer their paintings: actors, who make you sit, without a fag mind, through bizarre theatrical entertainments: scientists who invite you to visit their experiments. I got to prop up the kitchen wall at innumerable student parties, at least one of them quite good, as well as doing dinner parties, films, and, my very favourite, going round people's houses after the pub to smoke spliff and listen to old Lloyd Cole albums. Twice, I found myself building sandcastles on Lytham sands when I should have been attending lectures. And after three years of this life, I achieved a 2.1. I had proved that it was possible, even if you are the wrong side of 30, to take a reasonable degree and still to enjoy sex, drugs and rock 'n' roll. Well, not much sex to be frank, though I believe that other mature students were more fortunate than me. Here is a very good rule of thumb: if you spend as much time having fun as the 18 year-olds spend doing work, you won't go far wrong. And don't take it all too seriously.

Other Voices say:

"Generally, I've kept my friends that I had before I came here, and I don't have a campus social life. The mature student friends I had in the first year, we were all rushing about too much to spend any time in coffee bars, and when you did, it was all seriously depressing conversations about problems. In my second year, with the younger students, I've had to stop saying, "No, I can't come to this party," and "I'm sorry, but no I can't do that." They don't seem to realise that my life outside of University is totally different from theirs. I do go occasionally, and I do have a laugh, and I'm just amazed at their capacity for burning the candle at both ends. I could have a social life if I wanted, and I've been lucky to fall in with a group I like and who like me, and who do things that I enjoy, or am amused to watch them enjoy! It's as much a voyeuristic occupation; they're good to watch."

"I've made some really good friends, who I think will always stay friends. We get together once or twice a term and stay on campus and have a drink, or meet in the town where I live, but I can't stay late at night. I would like to have more of a social life. I come to concerts on campus occasionally and bring the children to things; I've made a point of that from the start. It's important to have some kind of social life. It can be very lonely coming back to full-time study, and everyone seems to know where they're going, and you do need someone to get through it with."

"I went to college at 18 and found the social life pretty limited. All activities seemed to centre around trying to get a boyfriend/girlfriend. If you just enjoyed dancing, drinking, listening to music and talking to people for their own sake, you were considered very weird! Coming back at 30 the search for love seems less intense and my ideal socialising becomes possible. I just have to remember to take time out to do some work!"

"I spend a good deal of time chatting in coffee bars - but it isn't always wasting time - having a good grumble is very therapeutic and I have actually had the odd good idea inspired by a friend and a cup of coffee. In fact, sometimes the conversation in the coffee bar is more useful than the seminar that preceded it!"

"Somehow I managed to fit a social life in with my degree. My friends are varied from ages 19 to 50; some undergraduates, some postgraduates and some workers; both women and men. I probably do less work because of my friends, but I probably enjoy the work I do more. I'm never quite sure how I manage to keep in touch with everyone, or they with me. Thank heavens for the telephone!"

Living on a Shoe-String

by

Stuart Rose

Deciding to become a mature undergraduate might be financially difficult but it's not impossible - I was surprised how I have been able to live on a grant and be relatively comfortable. If you haven't been to university before and are a single student under 50 years of age, you can get a mandatory grant which, including a student loan, is designed to cover all basic living and studying requirements. If you live in a partnership, you may still be eligible for a mandatory grant depending on your joint financial position. An informative booklet published by the Department of Education, Student Grants and Loans, summarises the current grant levels and all the ifs and buts. (In Scotland see Student Grants in Scotland, or in Northern Ireland see Awards and Loans to Students.) The mandatory grant can be increased for dependants, partners, and children - and for particular needs, for example, if you are disabled. You can get more information from your local authority who can be very helpful. However, authorities do vary and, as some of the grant permutations are complex, students can have problems agreeing their final award.

Every student's decision to come to university is different, and mine included being what some colleagues considered as financially reckless. I was getting to the top of a career, earning a large American-style remuneration package, and was mortgaged to the maximum. Most of what was left went on maintenance for my children. I chose to go to a particular university for the quality of its teaching staff which meant moving and selling my house at exactly the time when the housing market slumped. I realised in advance that by coming to university I would lose all my savings, so I wasn't surprised when it happened. All-in-all, my income plummeted from nearly £700 per week plus perks to £76 per week and no perks.

The question most mature students face is: how can I manage on a grant? The simple answer to this is that it is possible with careful budgeting and without the need for supplements. However, some students do augment their grant by working and at the local Job Centre there is usually a variety of jobs advertised on the 'Part-Time' and 'Temporary Work' notice boards. Under the terms of your grant you are allowed to earn up to your tax allowance without affecting your grant. At the Job Centre I found student-friendly work such as being a carer at an old people's home, earning £25 to £30 for a ten-hour shift overnight once a week; likewise a part-time cashier at a motorway service station gets £3 to £4 per hour. Evening bar work on- or off-campus may be available. Better paid work can be found working part-time at weekends selling houses for estate agents or developers. If you have been a teacher, you might be able to get occasional work marking exam scripts.

Alternative ways in which mature students make some extra money varies enormously. Some work full-time through the summer vacation, or take a year out (intercalate) in the middle of their studies to work and save. Some, with space in their homes, take in lodgers. Another idea to raise money, if you are in the process of buying your own house, is to sell it and buy a cheaper one. That way you might be financially more secure by reducing or even getting rid of mortgage repayments entirely, or by living off capital raised through the sale. Additionally, I found that a little extra money can be made by keeping my grant and student loan in a high interest building society account, only transferring it to a cheque account when it was required.

Accommodation expenses account for a major proportion of student expenditure. Fortunately, some university managed rooms, either on- or off-campus, come with the added benefit of no fuel bills. The off-campus accommodation office is a good source of advice on the availability and cost of local housing. Because of problems in selling my house, I did not know what money, if any, I would have in my first year at University. In these circumstances, I advertised in the local newspaper (successfully as it turned out) for free accommodation in return for undertaking do-it-yourself, domestic and other similar activities. Later, I wanted to live in the countryside; by sending a mailshot to local farmers, I managed to find cheap and peaceful rural accommodation.

There is help to be found on campus at the Student Welfare Offices if you get into real money difficulties during your course. A visit to their offices for advice on any financial matter is well worthwhile, even for relatively small matters - for example, how best to complete the annual financial statement for local authority grants. The welfare officers also advise on obtaining financial assistance from the Access Fund, which is a central government fund used at each university's discretion to help students in difficulty. Additionally, some university colleges will provide an emergency loan to students in need of immediate financial assistance. Banks, too, can be helpful by allowing students to run up sizeable loans to be repaid from work after their studies have finished.

Some students get caught out by the long summer but with planning you can avoid this. The grant cheque at the start of the Summer Term has to last until October, unless you can supplement it by vacation work. Obviously, it's not likely to last unless you have divided your total annual income by fifty-two weeks and budgeted accordingly. The weekly budget needs to cover the necessaries - rent, heating, food, books, transport, etc - plus the odd bottle of scotch and night out. This laborious process might sound tedious to do, but I found that organising my finances and planning for bills as far as possible in advance significantly reduced my problems of living on a shoe-string.

As a mature student, what might seem at first sight to be difficult financially can be, in reality, a lot less problematic than you might think. This view is supported by the fact that, every year, thousands of mature students manage their finances carefully, achieve their academic ambitions very successfully, and have great fun in the process. The ideas I have described in this chapter may help you to finance your way through three years' study, but they may not be possible or applicable to all. In fact, many students simply 'muddle through' quite successfully once having seen at the beginning of their studies that with grants, partners, savings, or any other source of funds, they will win through.

Other Voices say:

"Single parents can get income support over the summer (vacation) but it took the University Student Welfare Department to argue my case with the Department of Social Security."

"If your (ex-partner's) maintenance is more than your mortgage interest, you can lose some of your grant. So keeping a highish mortgage may be beneficial. Moving may not save you money."

"Not everyone is a financial entrepreneur, especially mature students with families and jobs. I think that people struggle one way or other at university. That's the lot of a mature student - struggle, struggle and more struggle. But it's worth it in the end."

"I had to have a face-to-face meeting with my Local Education Authority to sort out my grant. There are dependants' allowances available, and it's a case of being persistent and standing your ground. If you can, do some 'homework' beforehand so you have a good idea of your entitlements."

"I am absolutely hopeless at budgeting. I start out with good intentions but they go completely awry as soon as I put my grant cheque into the bank ... (yet) surprise, surprise, I survived financially."

"If you answer all those intrusive questions on the grant form creatively, you may not be as poor as you would be if you answered them as if you were studying for the church!"

Health, Ill Health and Disability

by

Sara Winterbourne

Looking back, I can't be sure where it all began, the slow inexorable descent into illness, but I remember vividly when I realised that I was in serious trouble, and that I would have to take my future into my own hands if I was to survive as a person, and as a student. It was clear by then that I could not do both at once. It is a truism that we take our (good) health for granted until it begins to disappear, and the effect this can have on daily life can be shocking. It can also be very revealing. These then are some reflections of my own experience of illness and subsequent disability, while simultaneously trying to achieve a good honours degree.

I struggled throughout my first year, feeling ill much of the time, with small oases of feeling myself again, when I would vainly try to catch up all the undone work. I had made myself attend all lectures and seminars, regardless of how I felt, so I had at least a skeleton of notes for the year's courses. Abandoning a convenient room on the campus for the undisturbed sanctuary of a rented house in the town, I worked my socks off for the three weeks before the end-of-year exams. Gaining high marks in all subjects, I was all set for the two years' work that counted towards the degree proper.

Midway through the Spring Term of the second year, I found myself being admitted to the Medical Centre in acute pain. Visited by fellow students, I was torn between the considerable warmth and support of my peer group, and the realisation that I couldn't fight any longer. Being ill and being a student had become mutually incompatible despite eighteen months of trying, and I was no nearer understanding what was in fact wrong with me. I had no choice about being ill, so I decided to tackle the other end of the problem. I knew that I could ask for a year off - an intercalation - while I could concentrate on finding out what was going on. I saw it as having the strength to face the realities of the situation and to find an intelligent solution. I arranged an interview with my Head of Department; his response was just what I needed. With relief, I accepted the breathing space. A year later, I returned little the wiser. My tutor greeted me with "Are you sure you're ready to come back. You look even worse than when you left last year!" Sadly he was right, and the intercalation was extended for a further year.

As I eventually picked up my studies again, the symptoms started to increase. The harder I worked, the more ill I felt. Tutors variously ascribed this to 'being a woman and therefore afraid of success', 'fear of failure' and 'everybody feels like their head is a block of concrete'. Beginning to believe in them rather than in my own experience, I struggled along. Then a lucky break! Attending a conference with friends on environmental health, I sneezed all the way through! Someone came up to me and said, "You must be allergic to something in this hall." To leap ahead, I ended up referring myself privately to a specialist - no mean feat on a student grant! The diagnosis was shocking - I was suffering from allergic reactions to food, airborne chemicals and other everyday allergens. Driving back up the M6 in heavy rain, and blinded by tears of relief and terror, I nearly precluded the need for any next step by pulling out in front of a long juggernaut.

A week later, I was in hospital for a month, in an environmental control unit, trying to track down exactly what it was I was reacting to. A month later I was banished to a place in Scotland, forbidden to come home until the gas appliances and gas supply, the new kitchen cupboards, and the new bedroom carpet were all removed, and the newly decorated and insulated walls stripped back to the bare plaster! At this point, a stone and a half lighter and in considerable pain as a result of the testing procedures, I applied again to the University to have another year's breathing space. A year later nothing had changed. A year later still the University, understandably, wrote to me to say that in view of the uncertain prognosis, it was felt that it was no longer appropriate to keep me on the books as an absent student, but that I should reapply should my situation change and this would be regarded with sympathy.

Three years later I was having an interview with a training agency regarding retraining opportunities. The occupational psychologist put it quite bluntly: no funds available. He suggested instead that I found something to occupy my very-active mind, so that I didn't add psychological break-down to the physical problems! I wrote to the University, and returned as a second year, part-time, unfunded (including fees), disabled student.

Going back as a part-time student, and taking a degree primarily by independent study and research, proved to be a good way of coping with the uncertainty of my daily health status. Furthermore, prompted by a suggestion made by the consultant immunologist, I revised my degree scheme to include much of what I had to learn about to understand what was happening to me, and how to become well again.

Three and a half years further on, life is looking good. Although it has been much harder than I could have anticipated, I have learned so much more than I ever expected to as a result of choosing to come to University more than a decade ago. I have learned just how supportive both individual people and the

University as an institution can be. Looking back, I realise that I usually turned up with a possible solution whenever I was presenting someone with a problem that I had to overcome, and I feel that tactic definitely encouraged people to help me. I have used the experience and knowledge gained over the years to feed back into my degree work, so that everything has become 'grist for the mill' for my studies. And I have learned that it is possible to survive all manner of things as a student, even if your life doesn't run smoothly to plan - and whose does?

Other Voices say:

"Intercalations are very important for mature students - if only knowing it's always there as an option."

"Although I've tried to stay healthy in my first year, I've still managed to catch a cold! I feel that many students can't afford to look after themselves properly, and maybe even don't know how to. It means that are a lot of bugs and illness around on the campus - and some people aren't immune to Lancaster."

"My own experience as a mature student with mild multiple sclerosis has been one of similar dogged determination to complete my degree course, preferably without a break. I have tried to attend every lecture and seminar, not only to try to get a good degree result, but because I didn't know what might happen next. With MS, remissions are often sudden, and can be temporarily or permanently catastrophic."

"Universities employ Disability Officers, so there's usually help available in varying degrees. I know of one student, for example, who developed tendonitis and so had quite severe problems writing. To help her, the university assisted in the temporary provision of a word processor. They also offered extra time in examinations, plus a choice in examination location of the computer centre or health centre."

"I think we do take our health for granted. But for many mature students being healthy themselves is not sufficient. Dependants must also be healthy. In my first year, two weeks before exams, I had to return to Yorkshire for a week or so to help my 70 year-old mother whilst my father was undergoing an operation. This drew on both my physical and emotional capacities, and then I had to go back to face my exams!"

"Having worked out of doors all my life until I came here, I'm a fairly healthy sort of chap. But that doesn't exclude you from any of the health problems that exist within the family. Because it was perceived that my being at the University was less important than my wife being at work, I've had to deal with all the family sickness that has happened, and change my routine accordingly."

Where To Go From Here?

by

Ian Marchant

There are certainly living examples of that fabulous beast, the mature student who has given up a rewarding, well paid career in order to scale the ivory towers of academia. This is how many lecturers see mature students; having themselves only ever lived and worked in these faintly medieval institutions, they hold anyone who has ever worked from nine to five in awe. But many mature students are ex-slackers, who, upon reaching some crisis in their lives, have decided upon a course of 'self-improvement', or 'getting qualified'. Although any number of mature students start with ideas about knowledge for its own sake, there will come a point, somewhere in your third year, where you will realise that your course is going to end quite soon, and, if you are not very careful, you will find yourself back in The Real World. The piece of paper for which you may have had a lofty and commendable disregard in your first and second years now begins to loom large in your mind. Soon, you will be 'qualified' to actually *do* something. But what?

It is at this stage that those sensible souls who decided to study something 'useful' like Management or Engineering will begin to feel a smug superiority. That's how I felt, applying for a place on an Engineering foundation course. "When all this is over, I'll be able to get a job!" Truth will out, however; I had no talent as an engineer, and kept asking the wrong questions, and I ended up coming to University to study History and Philosophy, subjects which, as I was informed by a cab driver, are "no use to society whatsoever". He's probably right. There is a contradiction between the ideals of the academic world and current government claptrap about 'the needs of employers' and the demands of the marketplace. At the beginning of your course, there is no doubt that ideals will take precedence over what putative employers may 'need' at some point in the future, but by the end, it is highly probable that you will be concerned about putting your degree to some use. This is unsurprising, but it is always worth remembering that a degree is something that you do for yourself, and for its own sake. It may not help you to find a job, but this does not matter, because that is not what degrees are for. They are not magic amulets which open employers' doors to the privileged few who have demonstrated their ability to write a few essays and sit a few exams, and nor should they be.

Here's what they tell you in the prospectus: employers think that the university experience changes people in a way which renders them useful as employees, so it does not matter what you have chosen to study. Ha! You may well feel that you have been in some way changed by university, but in Hard Times, which employer in her right mind is going to favour a 40 year-old ex-hospital porter with a First in Social Anthropology over a 21 year-old with a 2.2 in Business Studies? I do not believe that it is any harder for a mature student to take a degree than for anyone else, but it is undoubtedly much harder for us to find jobs. Another very real problem for graduating mature students is that they may be severely restricted in where they can go; they may have children in school, partners in work, mortgages, and other encumbrances which prevent them from upping sticks. My elder daughter is in a 'good school', which she hates; should I take her out of it, and off to a new place, or stick it out here, and hope she settles? A friend who relied on the support of her partner for the three years of her course, is embittered that graduating has not opened doors. It was her hope that she might become a high earner, and be able to take her family on holidays. And, for the year after graduation, she, like most of us, had no prospect of this at all. But ... a few months further on still, and all of my contemporaries are either in work, self-employment, or doing postgraduate courses. The year after graduation is almost always terrible; keep on keeping on, and things will improve out of sight.

Those mature students who have gained a professional qualification often do go straight from university into the 'job market' but if, like many mature students, you've studied a less straight-forwardly 'useful' subject, this may not seem like the next logical step. Many mature students have had a bellyful of the job market and the idea of a return to The Real World fills them with horror. That's one reason so many of our contemporaries end up as postgraduates, with funding if they are very lucky, and perhaps some teaching duties, but more often self-funded and part-time: in campus coffee bars across the land, many mature students fervently fill in applications for scholarships, but few are called. One friend, delighted to find that she had taken a First, was crestfallen to discover that even this did not guarantee postgraduate funding; her department, determined to hang on to her, managed to find her enough teaching to pay her fees, and to keep body and soul in relatively close proximity. A year of this hand-to-mouth existence, and she was offered a job, heading a newly formed department at a college of higher education; she now earns more than the tutors who taught her. Other friends have gone back part-time to the jobs that they had before they started as undergraduates, in order to fund postgraduate study. But, again, once through the 'year-after-graduation' barrier, and most have obtained teaching studentships. Others still, after a year and more of job-hunting, have decided to go in for teacher training. One friend said to me recently that he felt that teacher training should be added to death and taxes as unavoidable conditions of human existence, but he may be overstating his case. As my old Mum always says, "Worse things happen at sea."

There are any number of my acquaintances who have not really achieved much in life, and taking a degree is, for many of them, including me, the first thing that they have seen right through to the end. It was a valuable and rewarding experience, one of the most valuable and rewarding of my life to date. It gave me the confidence to start my own business (although not until, yes, you've guessed, a year after graduation). But it would be a mistake to see a degree as a passport to financial security. Maybe, after doing your degree, this will not be of concern. For me, it doesn't matter at all. I shape my own fate, and do not wish to be governed by 'the needs of employers', or the demands of the marketplace. Doing my degree as a mature student gave me the courage to recognise this fact.

Other Voices say:

"I live in Cumbria, and I don't think the family are going to move. I'm willing to cast the net quite wide, but I don't think I'm going to be able to get a much better job than I would before I came to University. It's still my ambition to work with others, as I used to, but maybe at a slightly higher level, for slightly better pay. I didn't come here for that; I'm here as a confidence building exercise."

"I don't know. I've absolutely no idea at all. When I leave here, I'm going to be 44, I'm going to have a degree of one sort or another, and half a lifetime of experience, but I don't know how it's going to fit into the modern job market. It doesn't worry me. I can find lots of other things to do with my life that I enjoy and are helpful for other people other than work for a wage. Apart from artificial status, and a few luxuries, working isn't that important. I'd be happy if I get a voluntary job with expenses paid. I don't need the status of a high earning job with a title."

"I saw the job advertised whilst I was working in the department on a placement as part of my degree. My immediate thoughts were, "Well, I don't finish until June, which is four months away; they won't be interested in me." I decided to apply, nevertheless, if only for the experience. I had an interview and they offered me the post: all I had to do was complete my degree (pass the CQSW) and I had a job. It was wonderful! I have been working for six months now. It's hard work but I thoroughly enjoy it. I still miss University, and looking back I realise what an easy life it was!"

"I left University with no confidence, no confidence at all. After about five months being unemployed, I got a short-term research job. I was delighted. On the same day I found out that I was pregnant: two great pieces of news on the same day. It was only when I had been doing the job for a little while that I got my confidence back. The contract was extended from the initial six months to a year and I thoroughly enjoyed the job. Now the research is finished and I am at home with my baby. At present I am looking for something part-time in primary health care, which is not too unlike what I was doing before I went to University. All I would say is you have to keep trying for jobs when you leave university. You cannot afford to give up hope."

"I saw this job in the daily paper, after being unemployed for a number of months. To my surprise, I was appointed. It's a fixed term contract, I don't know how much longer I'll have the job ... if there's no work, then they will finish some of us: I feel like I'm living on the edge. I'm not doing what I want to do, and I only do it for the money. To be honest, I don't think I would advise anyone with a good job to give it up for university; once you're out of the job market, things change so fast that it is hard to get back in. However, if you are like me and you have been out for a while with children, then it's a great way to get back into things."

The guidelines which follow have emerged during the production of this book; they are seen as techniques for improving the experience of academic life for mature students.

Recommendations for students

* Learn the 'Rules of the Game', the informal academic culture; work the system to your advantage: negotiate essay deadlines; use the Essay Bank kept by the Students' Union; be selective in material you read; learn how to skim books; find out how final degree classifications are structured.

* Build up formal and informal network structures; take time to talk to fellow students; share your own experiences as a learner, the struggles as well as the pleasures.

* Don't feel guilty; re-assess priorities; lower standards; learn how to compromise when the demands of academic work conflict with family responsibilities.

* Be flexible - rigid patterns don't always work.

* Don't do all the talking in your seminar groups; in discussion, try to find the right balance between personal experience and theory.

* Don't be too proud or frightened to ask for help; find out where to go for advice; do something about problems early on, before they become unmanageable.

* Don't take at face value claims made in prospectuses, especially in relation to child care provision and local housing markets.

* Have fun; don't take it all too seriously.

Recommendations for teaching staff

* Don't belittle the special needs and problems of mature students; accept that on occasions non-academic responsibilities might have to take priority over academic requirements; remember that a weekend's extension for an essay is worthless for a busy parent.

* Don't expect mature students to take the driving seat in seminar groups; try not to yawn when mature students start talking about their experiences.

Recommendations for academic institutions

* Regularly review administrative and academic practices in relation to mature students.

* Give consistent, accurate and up-to-date information to prospective students.

* Realise that mature students are not a homogeneous group; they're a mixed bunch of people with different needs to be accommodated.

* Encourage departments to adopt a positive approach concerning mature students.

* Think of possible implications for student-parents when time-tabling early morning and late afternoon lectures and seminars.

Notes on Contributors: What Happens Now? Have Our Intentions Changed?

As is clear from the paragraphs below, it is by no means uncommon for mature students to change their plans for the future during the course of their university career.

Hilary Arksey:

During my three years as an undergraduate my intentions to return to the 'real world' were gradually replaced by a wish to continue my studies. Being one of the fortunate ones to get funding, I am now half way through postgraduate studies. As for what I'll do if and when I'm allowed to join the 'Drs' club - well, I've always wanted to be a hairdresser!

Steve Barnes:

Coming up to the end of my first year, it is difficult to answer this question. However, during my first year opportunities have arisen and I am able now to expand on my initial ambition of becoming a qualified Social Worker with an Honours degree. I am thinking of postgraduate studies or maybe even teaching Social Work.

Lynne Boundy:

Now, two-thirds of my way through my degree, I feel a little like an escapee from the pages of 'The Women's Room'. My perceptions about university and the merits of a degree have altered. I now realise it's within the capabilities of most people to jump through the necessary paper hoops. On the other hand, I have learned to see the world through a different lens, to challenge assumptions I held, to recognise that tolerance for the rights and views of others is as important as commitment to one's own ideals. So, where do I go from here? There's a temptation to become the proverbial permanent student but I shall be happy simply to have achieved my ambition.

John Clarkson:

I came to University as a (very) mature student intent on reading English and Politics. Asked to choose a third subject for study, I opted (because of its intellectual image, rather than a raging thirst for 'Knowledge') to read Philosophy. By the start of my second year Philosophy had become an obsession and I had lost much of my enthusiasm for the other subjects. However, I knew that 'being a philosopher' was unlikely to improve my future employment prospects, and so chose to take a combined major in English and Philosophy, reasoning that this might increase my appeal to potential employers. During my third year, when 'The Future' suddenly seemed very close, I realised that I didn't really care what sort of job my nice new degree would qualify me for; I was enjoying university life and did not want it to end. So, now I'm taking an MA in Philosophy and, when I've got that, I intend to carry on and read for my PhD. After that? I don't know, but I can't honestly say that it worries me greatly. I came to University to achieve a personal goal; that done, my horizons have altered and so have I. If my dreams now turn out to have no 'practical' application to the job market then so be it. Learning to live without money is just one of many new skills acquired at university.

Ian Marchant:

Armed with my 2.1 in the History and Philosophy of Science, it took me a year to realise that no-one was going to give me a job, and that I could not face the thought of postgraduate work. But my old songwriting partner and I had been reunited, and we decided to form our own company to promote and release our songs. Negotiating with singers, studios and publishers, it took me some months to understand that I had left pop music, in order to go to university, and that, as soon as I left, I just went back to it again. Ho hum. And, fingers crossed, the single will be released in July...

Diane Nutt:

Here I am in the midst of my finals (literally, my third exam is tomorrow!) and I like being a student more than ever! So for me, what happens now? Well, I like the life so much I am staying on: I am becoming a postgraduate student. How has three years at university changed me? It has given me confidence, in myself and in my intelligence, and I have made friends. Most of all, however, I have learned that I want to share knowledge with others the way it has been shared with me.

Stuart Rose

My intentions have not changed. I still intend to carry out postgraduate research. Paths beyond that are now becoming more clear and I expect them to develop over the next three years. What has changed is the pressure. In the last few months of the final year, apart from finishing off coursework and preparing for exams - I need to get a First Class Honours degree to stand a chance of British Academy funding - I have had to sort out my PhD research topic, survey suitable universities and apply for a place, and apply for a postgraduate grant. So the last few months have become more serious and stressful. But this has to be offset against the sense of achievement when it's all over. If it had been easy, it would not have been worth nearly as much.

Cheryl Simmill:

When I first entered higher education I had no intention of going into postgraduate research. There were times when I wondered if I would survive as an undergraduate! However, it gradually dawned on me that three years would not be enough time to do all that I wanted to do; I had to confess to myself that I wanted to do further research.

To date it has not been easy. Even with a First there was no automatic funding. I worked part-time, on and off, to support my part-time, self-funded PhD. Happily, after a year I did get two and a half years' worth of funding from the Science and Engineering Council and that's what is keeping me going - for now.

Sara Winterbourne:

My life has become my work in more ways than one. I am now completing my professional training as a counsellor, and, as part of my training, have been working in a doctor's surgery with clients trying to make sense of their lives, especially when confronted with illness. This in turn is feeding back into my work as a student. So here I am twelve years on, still pursuing the Holy Grail of a degree, still full of enthusiasm and optimism. A very different degree from the one I started out on, as I am a <u>very</u> different person from the 30 year-old who started this. One of these years it will happen - I will be walking up onto that platform in a mortarboard and gown, finally a graduate.